Shells

*A Cameo of
Anne Morrow Lindbergh*

A play by
Virnell Ann Bruce

Copyright © 2008 by Virnell A. Bruce
All rights reserved

"Shells — A Cameo of Anne Morrow Lindbergh" is the sole property of the author and is fully protected by copyright. All rights, including but not limited to, professional, amateur, motion picture, recitation, lecturing, public reading, radio broadcast, television, video or sound taping, and the rights of translating into foreign languages, are strictly reserved.

No part of this publication may be reproduced or transmitted in any form or by any means, electronic or mechanical, including photocopy, recording or any other information storage or retrieval system now known or to be invented, without permission in writing from the publisher, except by a reviewer who wishes to quote brief passages in connection with a review written for inclusion in a magazine, newspaper, or broadcast. In its present form, the play is dedicated to the reading public only.

Printing by Farmville Printing

ISBN 978-0-9797787-0-4

Moon Shells Publishing

P. O. Box 6716
Williamsburg, Virginia 23188

Preface

Anne Morrow Lindbergh came from great wealth, married the world's most famous hero, was a pioneering aviator, and was a significant writer of the twentieth century. And yet, not many people know much about her life, other than she had a baby who was kidnapped and she wrote *Gift from the Sea.* In *Shells,* she has tea with a guest and tells the story of her life, from her early years reading and writing in her diary — through the death of her husband Charles and her adjustment to widowhood.

In telling her story, Anne not only describes the best part of her marriage — their pioneering flights around the world in a single-engine airplane — but reveals the difficult years of her marriage, including Charles' frequent absences and his unrelenting criticism. The story of their lives includes impressive book successes as well as personal affairs for both of them. Anne honestly describes her affair with a trusted friend — and painfully confides her devastating discovery of another family that Charles had in Germany.

Shells

Throughout her life, Anne got through the difficult periods and celebrated the happy times by writing: journals, letters, books and articles. In *Shells*, she describes not only the special places where she wrote, but the special people who influenced her writing. Her life became literature, from the time she was a newlywed, facing the tragic death of her baby — to the agonizing middle years, when she wrote her most famous book — to her years of widowhood, facing life alone. Anne continuously worked to find her true self and become a whole person through the growth of her heart, mind and spirit.

During this personal journey, Anne was on a constant quest to find what she called Real Life. As *Shells* unfolds, it's evident she needn't have gone looking for Real Life — it found her.

I had tea with Mrs. Lindbergh at her home in Darien, Connecticut, in November 1996. I vividly remember the large fireplace adorned with French crystal boxes, the bench coffee-table loaded with books, the sculpture of her as a young woman, and a great view of the river and sound. And, like so many people, I had seen numerous family photographs over the years, but at one point I thought, "Oh my goodness, those are the *originals!*" I was thrilled just to be in the company of someone for whom I had such great admiration and respect. I am eternally grateful to my faithful friend Susan Flowers for taking me with her on that afternoon, because it proved to be a priceless experience and an invaluable inspiration.

We took Mrs. Lindbergh a large florist's bouquet of pink flowers as well as a bouquet of colorful fall leaves and pine branches we picked up along the road. She kept admiring the natural bouquet. I also gave her a rose harp shell. "Oh," she exclaimed holding it gingerly, "it's *beau*tiful."

I would like to thank Reeve Lindbergh for her gracious consideration and always taking time out of her busy life to respond to my requests. As she does in her own writing, she provided insightful information about her mother in an open and honest way.

I would also like to note that after all my research, I do not believe Mrs. Lindbergh knew the details about Charles' German children. However, by the time I decided to write the play, the whole world knew about his indiscretions, so I had to include the information, which ultimately only makes her story more interesting.

And, indeed, it is a story worth telling.

Virnell Ann Bruce

Acknowledgments

The author is grateful for all of the permissions granted, for production as well as print.

Excerpts from *North to the Orient; Listen! the Wind; The Steep Ascent; Dearly Beloved; Bring Me a Unicorn — Diaries and Letters, 1922-1928; Hour of Gold, Hour of Lead — Diaries and Letters, 1929-1932; Locked Rooms and Open Doors — Diaries and Letters, 1933-1935; The Flower and the Nettle — Diaries and Letters, 1936-1939; War Within and Without — Diaries and Letters, 1939-1944;* by Anne Morrow Lindbergh, used with permission by Harcourt.

Excerpts from *Gift from the Sea,* by Anne Morrow Lindbergh, used with permission by Random House.

Excerpts for production from *No More Words — A Journal of My Mother, Anne Morrow Lindbergh, The Names of the Mountains,* and *Under A Wing,* by Reeve Lindbergh, used with permission by Reeve Lindbergh.

Excerpts from *Autobiography of Values* and *The Wartime*

—————————— *Shells* ——————————

Journals of Charles A. Lindbergh, by Charles A. Lindbergh, used with permission by Harcourt.

Excerpts from *Lindbergh,* by A. Scott Berg, used with permission by the Penguin Group of G. P. Putnam's Sons as well as by A. Scott Berg.

Excerpt from *Airman's Odyssey,* by Antoine de Saint-Exupery, used with permission by Harcourt.

Excerpts from *Special People,* by Julie Nixon Eisenhower, used with permission by Julie Nixon Eisenhower.

Excerpts from a television interview between Eric Sevareid and Anne Morrow Lindbergh, 1977, used with permission by CBS News.

Excerpts from a television interview between Morley Safer and Anne Morrow Lindbergh, "60 Minutes," April 20, 1980, used with permission by CBS News.

Excerpts from *Anne Morrow Lindbergh: Her Life,* by Susan Hertog, used with permission by Susan Hertog.

Quote from *Letters to a Young Poet,* by Rainer Maria Rilke, used with permission of W. W. Norton & Company.

Shells

Act One

SETTING: *The Lindbergh home in Darien, Connecticut. Upstage center is a fireplace, with a large desk in corner, stage right, surrounded by windows. The desk has books, flowers, a pair of binoculars and a basket. Center stage is a large chair next to a table. A table sits stage right and is covered with photographs. A bench sits beside it. A small writing desk sits upstage left with a straight chair behind facing out. Blue paper, a tablet, books, a tray of pencils, a basket, shells and feathers sit on desk.*

It is May 1980. Music up: Bach, Concerto in E, Allegro. ANNE MORROW LINDBERGH enters, stage left. She carries a tea service and puts it on the table center stage. Comes downstage.

ANNE. *(To audience)* It's quite cool outside. I've made some tea. It'll take the chill off from my daily walk. Perhaps you'll join me? Oh, how nice. I don't have guests very often, so this is quite special. *(Pause.)* What a lovely spring day. I always enjoy my walks, especially when I can watch nature unfold again. I've savored thirty-four springs here in Scott's Cove. It's the best place in Connecticut to live with nature and watch her grow and change every year. I enjoy the constant cycle of life each day, right in my own back yard.

(She takes off shawl and puts on back of chair. Turns to windows, stage right.)

From here, I watch the ducks, geese, sparrows — sometimes a swan or a cardinal. I feed them every day. Occasionally, I see raccoons in the driveway — or turtles near the water — *(mock anger)* or deer eating my flowers! I'm especially fond of that red squirrel. I wonder if they know they're special, just as I wonder if some people know how special *they* are. *(Comes downstage.)* My neighborhood is a kind of church, and feeding the birds every day is a kind of prayer — heartfelt and sacred to me. It feeds *my* spirit.

This home is my personal nest. When Reeve — the youngest of our children — left for college, my husband and I decided to shed that large, sturdy shell of a house next door and build this much smaller one. Then six years ago — in 1974 — my husband died. So now I live here with my memories — and my future. But I'm ahead of myself. Oh, I think the tea is ready. *(Pause.)*

(Sits in chair, center stage.)

Afternoon teatime has always been important to me. When I was a child, my mother would stop everything she was doing each day at five o'clock and read to us.

Shells

When we were older, we used that time to read or write in our diaries. It began my life-long love affair with words and communication. My diary is nearly 70 years old! It's a marvelous tool for a writer — or an observer of life. It's a way to look inward to your personal insight. What you really think. And, over the years, you can see how your inward journey has evolved. *(Pours tea.)* I've continued that five o'clock tradition, taking a few moments to enjoy tea — maybe some cookies — and give balance to my day.

Mother also read to us in the evenings — everything from *Little Women* to Greek mythology. Always the advocate of education. She was at Smith when she met my father when he was working his way through Amherst. I grew up in their polite and gentle world. It was a world that kept me separated from many aspects of life. So I've been on a constant search for Real Life — the kind of life that doesn't come from privilege. *(Pause.)* Growing up, we went to the best schools — and traveled extensively. We benefited in many ways from our parents' abundance. *(Laughing.)* I think all of us moved in and out of their home in New Jersey whenever we needed a place to stay between life's other destinations. *(Pause.)*

Oh, how mother loved that house. We called it Next Day Hill. We hadn't been there a month when mother was the proud hostess of a New Year's Eve party for nearly a thousand people. *(Amused.)* She was in her element that night. *(Rises.)* She also loved our apartment in New York. It was grand — we had a handsome ballroom — and a marvelous view of Central Park.

―――――――――――――― *Shells* ――――――――――――――

(Goes to table, stage right.)

My two sisters and I all went to Smith College. Actually, I wanted to go to Vassar, because I wanted to find my own identity, rather than be someone's daughter or niece or sister at Smith. But, parental pressure won out. *(Picks up photo. Talks to mother.)* Mother, we all knew your real love affair was with Smith. They returned your affection — with that honorary Doctorate — and making you acting president. But with all your community service and your extensive travel — you were so often inaccessible.

(Returns photo. Goes to stage left. Pause.)

It was at Smith that I began to realize my true passion for writing — and my ability to find myself through writing. It's a long and difficult journey to find one's self. In college, I published poems, essays and stories. *(Proudly.)* When I graduated, I won the two most prestigious prizes for writing at Smith. I was shy and had little confidence then, so I hardly believed it — but I did enjoy the recognition.

I've also spent a great deal of my life writing letters. I've probably written thousands. It's a solitary activity. But in my family, an experience was not finished until it was written down — or shared with someone. Only then is the experience truly alive. So, I learned very early to observe and express myself in writing. *(Pause.)*

I came from a world where education was valued above

Shells

all else, a world of books and letters. One that hardly prepared me for a life filled with action. *(Pause)*

(Goes to center stage.)

My life began the day I met Charles Lindbergh. Oh, I was born 21 years before that — when Teddy Roosevelt was president and just three years after the Wright brothers' flight at Kitty Hawk. *(Pause.)* We met in Mexico City at Christmas time. My father had just become Ambassador to Mexico and needed to improve relations between our countries, so he invited Charles to fly down on a goodwill trip. Of course, by then he was an international hero.

If you think my mother was accomplished, you should have met my father. His impeccable credentials were welcome all over the world. President Coolidge made him chairman of his Aircraft Board to study aviation; so one night the President, my father and Charles had dinner together. When father became Ambassador, he invited Charles to fly The Spirit of St. Louis to Mexico City. And we met. *(Pause.)*

(Goes to table stage right and picks up photo of Charles.)

I remember the first time I saw him. *(Muses.)* He's so tall — and good-looking — but with a shy demeanor, and a sensitive appearance — not like those grinny photos in the newspapers. Oh, those piercing blue eyes! And that *unmistakable* dimple in his chin. *(Returns photo.)*

─────────── *Shells* ───────────

I was smitten! So I watched him. I instinctively knew where he was in the room, partly because he was so tall, but also because I could just sense his presence. Those were the days when I wished I were more like my older sister Elisabeth. She was perfect — graceful and skillful, like a swan taking flight.

(Goes to center stage.)

My mother warned us that Charles had more publicity and attention than he wanted, so we should be quiet and just listen. Well, you can imagine *me* there — the most shy, self-conscious person ever — with two terribly accomplished parents, an older sister who was absolutely perfect, and the most sought-after man in the world. I felt totally inadequate! *(Laughing.)* Of course I kept quiet! Didn't say a word. And, he remembered me because of that.

That week, Charles found time to take my whole family flying in a Ford Tri Motor. Like most people, I had never been flying before. Oh, it was heaven! A complete and intense experience — *(Smiles.)* even before I wrote about it in my diary. I sat behind Charles and kept one eye on the scenery and one eye on him. *(Pause.)* That week changed my life. *(Ponders.)* I remember when I was graduating from high school — we had to fill out a questionnaire that asked, "What is your life ambition?" *(Smiles.)* I answered, "I want to marry a hero." And so, I had met a true hero.

It took Charles ten months to call. Of course everyone —

─────── *Shells* ───────

especially me — thought he would be calling Elisabeth. My two sisters and I had all fallen in love with him. I could hardly believe it when he called *me* that October morning. There I was with the telephone, paralyzed. "Hello?" *(As Charles.)* "Hello. This is . . . Lindbergh himself."

We went flying on our first date and within a week, were engaged.

(Goes to small bench, stage right. Sits)

(Laughs.) Yes, my parents were stunned. When we were in Mexico City, my father actually promoted Charles to us. Talked about him in glowing terms; said he didn't drink or womanize. When he found out we wanted to get married, he began to worry. *(Amused.)* He kept saying, "Well, what do we know about this man Lindbergh?" My parents thought we should think about it for a while. After all, I had not had a serious relationship before — and Charles had never dated anyone! I came from a sheltered life of books, and he came from a life of action.

The only thing we had in common was youth. Well, in an odd way, we had writing. *(Smiling.)* I told him I wanted to write, and he said, *(As Charles:)* "Well, I want to do the things people write about!" After we announced our engagement, my mother said, *(As mother:)* "Anne, you'll have the sky!" And, indeed, I did. *(Pause.)*

Ever since I met Charles, I've felt an inexplicable connection to him. I thought he believed in me and what I

Shells

could do, and so I found I could do more than I realized. He opened the door to Real Life — and drew me in. He was my moon — a powerful attraction that pulled at my hopes and dreams — and carried me to wherever he was, and wherever he was going. When I married him, I didn't expect happiness — but a life where I could stretch and grow. And — I had my hero. *(Pause.)*

Only twenty-two people attended our wedding at Next Day Hill. *(Looks at photos on table.)* All of these photos, and not one from my wedding. I've always regretted that, but we were so paranoid then, we kept everything secret and wouldn't dare ask a photographer in. *(Walks to center stage.)* For our honeymoon, we borrowed a powerboat and went to Penobscot Bay in Maine, where my parents had a marvelous house on North Haven Island. We even hiked on Big Garden Island, a delightful little retreat my father gave us as a wedding present. *(Pause.)*

That trip exposed me to a phenomenon that haunted us for years. Stalking. As a hunter carefully pursues his prey. The press found us and began tailing us like we were escaped convicts. One reporter circled our boat for eight hours! Charles was the first person to be truly stalked by the press — and from then on, I received the same treatment. It was frightening.

Charles was the most famous person in the world then — and was celebrated beyond imagination. Maybe you were one of the millions of people who saw his ticker-tape parade in New York — or wrote him a letter. He received hundreds of awards. The Congressional Medal of Honor. The first Distinguished Flying Cross. He was Time Magazine's first Man of the Year.

Throughout all of that, I think he maintained great personal integrity. He refused dozens of opportunities to make millions of dollars — endorsements for toys, cereals, calendars, zippers, hats — you name it! *(Laughing.)* Even William Randolph Hurst wanted him to star in a movie with Marion Davies. *(Pause.)*

Instead, he used his hero status to promote aviation. Up until that Paris flight, aviation in America was considered more as entertainment — like the circus. Charles helped lead its transition. He spent three months flying the *Spirit of St. Louis* to all 48 states, reaching more than 30 million people, with speeches and parades in 80 cities. That's when America's aviation industry took flight. Hero, indeed.

(Goes to chair, center stage. Drinks tea.)

Of course, all that took place before we even met. After we were married, I helped him. Charles consulted for Transcontinental Air Transport and worked very hard to ensure their inaugural trip between New York and Los Angeles was perfect. I went along to encourage people that flying was safe and fun. *(Amused.)* It was really something. You didn't fly at night then, so the route was a combination of railroad and airplane travel.

———————————— *Shells* ————————————

First, you would get on the train in New York and go to Columbus. You would fly from Columbus to Oklahoma. There, you would get on an overnight train to New Mexico. In the morning, you would fly to Los Angeles, making a stop in Arizona. *(Laughs.)* This was in record time, of course! It only took 48 hours! *(Pause. Stands.)*

The time Charles and I spent flying together was pure gold. We had so many marvelous experiences. Well, except for my lessons. He would make me land — and land — and land — and land that airplane until I set it down perfectly. It was pretty exasperating, but I had to live up to his expectations. The first time I soloed, I flew from Long Island — over Manhattan — to Newark. Oh, I felt like a queen! I learned to navigate using a sextant, a few charts — and the moon, the sun and the stars. There was no voice radio, so I learned Morse code. It was truly thrilling. I was desperate to do all this as well as a man could. And I did.

Charles wanted to chart some air courses. So he ordered a Lockheed Sirius built to his specifications. *(Amused.)* For Charles, outlining the specifications for an airplane was very much like outlining those for a wife. When he was considering marriage, he wanted *(sternly)* good health, good form, good sight and hearing — and from a healthy family. He said his experience from growing up on a farm taught him the importance of good heredity. *(Pause.)*

In the Sirius, he wanted a tandem cockpit with dual controls — and electrified flying suits to keep us warm. *(Goes to bench, stage right, sits down.)* While we were in California to pick up that plane, I became the first woman to earn a glider pilot's license. It's frightening to be pulled off that hill all alone. But as soon as I was airborne, it was close to heaven — with extraordinary silence and that unbelievable power of the air.

We finally picked up our new Sirius and returned to New York on Easter Sunday — and, with one stop, broke the transcontinental speed record by three hours. Oh, was I glad to get home! I was seven months pregnant and exhausted after nearly 15 hours in that small plane. *(Pause.)*

Flying in those early days was tremendously exciting. It gave me limitless horizons — and the beginnings of self-confidence. And unlike flying today, it gave me a wonderful sense of the earth, to feel a part of it. When I wasn't busy at my duties or enjoying the tapestry of the earth, I recited poetry — or memorized poems. Sometimes, Charles and I would exchange notes. When he wanted to say something to me, he would pull the plane up into a stall and throttle down the engine. *(Stands. Excitedly.)*

Occasionally we experienced that special rainbow phenomenon. Perhaps you've seen it? When you're in the clouds there's a complete, small circle of a rainbow riding along beside you — and in the center is the shadow of your plane. It's marvelous. *(Pause.)* And every time you land, you are reborn to the earth. *(Pause.)*

Shells

Of course, Charles was the consummate pilot. For him, flying was comfortable and familiar. Getting into the cockpit was like pulling on a favorite sweater. I could pick him out in the air just by the way he banked the plane. He knew exactly where that edge was, and he could maneuver right up to it. I always felt safe with Charles at the controls. Many of his contributions are still appreciated today, like the weather stations across the country or the safety check list. Oh, he was known for his detailed lists: equipment, maps, landmarks, weather forecasts. He had lists for everything.

(Goes to center stage.)

(Pause.) My life certainly began a new stage when I married Charles. I've often said that a woman's life changes about every twenty years. Not everyone goes through all the stages, but they're certainly true in my life. There are twenty years of growing up, eventually leaving the protective shell of your parents' home. Then there are twenty years of marriage and young children and becoming your own person. *(Pause.)*

In my second stage, I traveled extensively. Especially when I was newly married. It was a nomadic life — to and from cities and states and countries. A constant expedition across oceans and continents. And throughout the feverish outward journey, I faced a continuous struggle to understand and navigate my inward journey — to find myself. To become whole. *(Pause.)*

Shells

My first baby was born two months after returning from that California trip — in June 1930. *(Smiles.)* Yes, it was close, but I didn't know any better. We were living back at Next Day Hill, where mother had set up a delivery room and nursery. But new motherhood didn't last very long. My precious little Charlie was just a year old when we went on our first survey trip. But I wanted to be with my husband more than anything in the world, so I left my child behind to join the adventure.

(Goes to bench, stage right, sits.)

Charles wanted to find the shortest route from New York to Tokyo. He had pontoons put on our Sirius and pre-positioned fuel along the route. So after great planning — and many lists — off we went. There were breath-taking moments looking down on territory that no one had ever seen before. *(Stands up.)*

One of the proudest moments in my life happened on that trip. *(Very animated.)* Charles was having a rather heated discussion with some men on our first stop in Canada about our route, which they thought was unsafe. They suggested another route. One man said, "I wouldn't take my wife over that territory," Charles looked at me and said, "You have to remember, she's crew." It was a proud moment for me. *(Pause.)*

There were many times when I was truly afraid. Terrified, really. "Oh Charles, I thought we were going to *die*!" He said everyone feels fear; it was just easier for him because

─────────────── *Shells* ───────────────

he was actively in control of the airplane. Charles was always in control, even of fear. *(Pause.)* Sometimes we'd have to make a quick landing in bad weather — *(very animated, winding)* so I had to reel in the antenna as fast as I possibly could — one-hundred and fifty turns — so it didn't drag or break off when we landed. *(Laughs.)* So often I just barely made it. *(Pause.)*

We were in China when we received word that my father had died, so we returned to Next Day Hill. *(Picks up photo of father.)* Oh, father, you left us so suddenly. I was devastated. I still miss you. He was only 58, but was so accomplished. Many people thought he'd be the Republican presidential candidate in 1932. *(Returns photo. Pause.)*

(Goes to center stage.)

I was glad to be home. I had been away from little Charles for more than three months. I ached for him and dreamt about him almost every night. I missed his first haircut — and his first steps. It was terribly painful for me to be away so much. We stayed at my mother's house at first, which was fine with me since I was pregnant again and a bit nauseated. *(Cheerful.)* It's wonderful to have a staff of servants when you're pregnant. *(Pause.)*

When our house in Hopewell was nearly complete, we went there on weekends. *(Sadly.)* And then, as the whole world knows, on March first of 1932, my baby was kidnapped. And my life changed forever. We exhausted every avenue to find him, including some terribly strange

_____ *Shells* _____

detours. After that first night, I didn't really believe I would ever see him again — but I couldn't stop hoping. After ten agonizing weeks, my mother broke the news to me. "Anne, the baby is with Daddy." Little Charles died that night as he was taken from our house — confirming what I felt all along. *(Pause.)*

Losing a child is like amputation — a part of you dies. And so there's a part of me that is gone forever. My suffering was in solitude. Charles couldn't tolerate my sadness or tears, so I cried alone when he was gone, usually off running the kidnapping investigation. It's a desperate feeling — to mourn alone. I think Charles had his own way of dealing with the tragedy. But he never discussed it. Ever. And to this day, I'm painfully disappointed that I never saw him cry over the death of our baby. Not once. *(Pause.)*

Little Charles was born on my twenty-fourth birthday. *(To baby Charlie.)* Oh, Charlie. I've always treasured our shared birthday — it's brought me such comfort. You would be 50 years old next month. It's hard to believe we've privately celebrated our life together that long. Our own personal communion — especially on our birthdays. You were such a sweet baby and brought me such true joy. You still blaze within me. *(Pause.)*

Even now I draw the drapes every night for protection from someone seeing inside and watching. Someone *must* have known we were home and watched us that night. The thought still sends a chill right through me.

Shells

My husband always believed the press was responsible for our baby's death; they constantly and relentlessly stalked us. When little Charles was born, we didn't release any information, so they started printing stories that he was deformed — or stillborn. Even after we provided the name and a photo, they continued to stalk us. *(Pause. Sad.)* Even when little Charles was in the morgue — the morgue — a photographer broke in and took a picture — *(Lights flash like camera flash. ANNE puts arms up to shield eyes.)* and sold copies. I couldn't bear it.

Charles never trusted the press. Over the years, he became pretty irrational about them. Oftentimes, he even used a disguise to avoid notice. I'm not sure we had to be as cautious as we were, but Charles always *thought* we had to be. *(Pause.)* It was after the kidnapping when Charles first warned me against putting anything in writing that I wouldn't want seen on the front page of a newspaper — or saying anything that I wouldn't want shouted from the housetop. Those are paralyzing thoughts for a writer.

We no longer wanted to live in Hopewell, so of course we moved in with mother. She even added a wing to her house for us. Shortly afterward, my second baby was born. *(Smiles.)* It was a perfect baby boy. Jon's birth broke the spell over me. Life had been given back and my faith was reborn. And once again, I was thrilled he had that unmistakable dimple in his chin. *(Pause.)*

(Goes to bench, stage right.)

―――――――――――― *Shells* ――――――――――――

Less than a year later we were off on another expedition. Just as I was settling into motherhood. I felt terrible I was going to miss Jon's first birthday. But I just couldn't say no to Charles. He expected me to be with him to share his pursuits. *(Pause.)* This time we went in the other direction, a full circle around the Atlantic. *(Points around.)* Greenland. Iceland. Europe. Africa. South America. The Caribbean. *(Pause.)*

Our airplane got its name on that trip: Tingmissartoq. We were in Greenland when Charles was returning from a flight. As I watched him land, I saw some Eskimo children pointing to the plane and shouting, "Tingmissartoq! Tingmissartoq!" It's their language for "the one who flies like a big bird."

We spent an extra three weeks exploring Greenland. It was then I realized I couldn't determine exactly when we'd get home. Charles never could be pinned down to a schedule. Throughout his life, he stumbled around the globe like a dog sniffs around a neighborhood. He thought the Atlantic trip was really the high point of his career in aviation, and in some ways more demanding than his flight to Paris. We faced incredible danger, with times of sheer terror for me. *(Sits. Pause.)*

There was a point where the struggle to return was so great I wasn't sure we ever would. After many attempts to chart a path across the Atlantic to South America, we finally made it to Bathurst, on the west coast of Africa. We began to prepare the airplane for the trip. Weight was

Shells

always an issue. And wind. Wind was absolutely essential — and yet — it was so unpredictable.

We had to leave at night in order to arrive at the other end — an area unknown to us — in daylight. We started out the first night with a nearly full moon, our only light. "All set?" Charles would always say before takeoff. "All right," I always replied. We tried to take off for two nights. But the air was too dense and too still — and the aircraft too heavy. *(Pause.)* We finally had to leave behind everything that wasn't necessary — clothes, camera, emergency food, tools, cans of oil. Even the anchor. Charles took cutters and carefully snipped out an empty gas tank.

We were anxious on the third night because it was our last chance and there was little wind. *(Stands.)* The moon marked the path as we taxied out into the bay. As we swung around, the wind was rising. "All set?" "All right." *(Excited, animated. Engine noise begins, low.)*

Along we went, faster and faster, taking what seemed like forever. The spray enveloped us, curling over the wings — we couldn't see the tips. The plane wobbled up and down, side to side, as we kept spanking and spanking and spanking the tops of the waves. The engine sputtered. I thought there was something wrong with it and was surprised when we continued on, surely facing death. But finally, finally we were . . . ever . . . so . . . slowly . . . rising, smoothing out along the way. Ah, what joy! We climbed up and up — away from the lights and into the darkness toward Brazil. *(Engine noise grows, cuts out. Pause.)*

―――――――――― *Shells* ――――――――――

By moonlight, I recorded the takeoff at two o'clock Greenwich Mean Time. Then I radioed South America to let them know we were on our way, and transmitted our position every fifteen minutes — for sixteen hours. We averaged an altitude across the Atlantic of about a thousand feet. A few hours into the flight, I made contact with a station in Massachusetts! Thousands of miles away. It was absolutely thrilling. And — while it did set the distance record for communication between an airplane and a ground station — they asked for a newspaper interview! *(Amused.)* I told them I was just too busy and had to get back to work. *(Pause.)*

We flew through some heavy storms on that part of the trip. Flying blind always brought on sheer terror for me, and I really struggled to overcome the fear of death. Now there's Real Life. But I always trusted Charles. And, of course being together and sharing the experiences — whether pleasant or fearful — brought us closer together. *(Pause.)*

When Charles spotted a ship, he'd rock the plane to get my attention. I contacted one ship and we dropped down to say "Hello." The radio operator said they'd see us from the port side, so there they were — all lined up, waving at us. I was *(waving, very animated)* waving frantically in return, thrilled with just the basic communication. As we flew away, they radioed Christmas greetings.

My goodness. Christmas. It was then that overwhelming weariness took hold of me. I was desperately homesick and felt an intense longing for my baby. I knew I met Charles' expectation to be with him, but still, I wondered why I had left Jon for so long. Charles always was persuasive. I was hoping we'd be home for Christmas with little Jon. Well, after traveling nearly 30,000 miles in six months, we made it. *(Pause.)*

(Moves to stage center.)

Tingmissartoq was a wonderful aircraft. It transported us to different lands and exotic cultures. My familiar station in the cockpit was a warm and protective shell. It's where time stood still. I became quite connected to that cockpit. After all, we shared many emotional experiences: great joy, intense fear, hours of pleasure. Tingmissartoq always brought us home safely. *(Pause.)*

We were living at Next Day Hill when Charles ordered a new airplane. We picked it up in St. Louis on our way to California to see my sister Elisabeth. For years, she had been seriously ill with heart disease. We were there only a couple of days when Detective Schwarkzopf called to say they arrested the man who they thought had kidnapped our baby. So we left early to prepare for the trial. Less than three months later, Elisabeth died. We all painfully knew she was mother's favorite, especially when she asked: *(As mother.)* "Of all my children, why did it have to be Elisabeth?" *(Pause.)*

Three years. Three deaths. It was too much to bear, and I felt very alone and isolated. The trial began only one

Shells

month after Elisabeth died. The Trial of the Century. It was also theater at its best. And worst.

(Goes to chair, center stage.)

(Lights flash as a camera flash.) There I was, on the witness stand, talking about my baby. I vividly remember my testimony, providing information about that night: little Charlie's clothing, the shear panic when we couldn't find him. On the outside, I appeared calm and controlled. On the inside, I struggled with the pain and suffering all over again. It was dreadful. *(Pause.)* Hundreds of reporters filled the courtroom and the town for weeks. Newspaper sales soared. Sixty thousand tourists showed up one weekend just to see the courtroom. Celebrities came — as though it were entertainment!

Eighty seven witnesses contributed to the death sentence, and Bruno Hauptman was executed the next year. *(Quizzingly.)* But you know, he never confessed to the crime, even though it meant a great deal of money for his wife and a lesser sentence for himself.

(Sadly. Distracted.) I am aware — painfully aware — that there have been many theories about the kidnapping over the years. But if they reopened the case, they would have to re-examine all the evidence — the events. I wouldn't be able to face that, to experience that again. It was all too excruciating. Once was more than enough for my lifetime. I haven't read any of the books with other theories and — I don't intend to. *(Pause. Stands.)*

―――――― *Shells* ――――――

Death was all around me then. I was constantly dreaming of my son, my father and my sister. I would wake up crying. It was an especially dark period in my life, and I was dangerously fragile. *(Pause.)*

(Goes to desk at stage left.)

And so I wrote. To tell my story. To soothe my soul. To make sense of life and its experiences. To breathe. The habit of writing almost daily helped me immensely and probably saved my sanity. I could literally see what I thought and felt in my own words. My sorrow helped me to write with greater honesty.

I connected my need to write with my experiences from those survey trips. No one had ever flown to many of the places we went, so no one had the perspective the trips gave me. As I wrote, I re-observed the people and places — and, I searched for my own personal meaning of the inward journey from the events of the outward journey.

(Sits down in chair.)

My first book was *North to the Orient*. The acclaim and awards given to that book were duplicated when *Listen! the Wind* came out three years later. I had finally established myself in my own world — the writing world. *(Proudly.)* I was considered as good a writer as Charles was a pilot. The success gave me immense personal satisfaction — and validated my inward journey. *(Smiles.)* I was sure this was part of Real Life. *(Pause.)*

Throughout this time, the press continued to stalk us. Relentlessly. Then one day, something happened that changed our lives. *(Stands. Very animated.)* A teacher was driving Jon home from school when another car forced them over to the side of the road. A man jumped out and pushed a camera into little Jon's face. *(Lights flash and pop as a camera flash.)* He was just a child. The situation had been intolerable for years, so it didn't take Charles long to make up his mind. We took flight, this time on a ship.

(Pause. Goes to stage center.)

We lived in Europe for more than three years — traveling extensively and meeting a countless array of truly fascinating people. *(Pause.)*

Our first home was in the country about an hour outside London. An old, rambling cottage called Long Barn. It had stunningly beautiful gardens with abundant flowers. The area provided privacy for luxurious walks with Charles and Jon — something we couldn't do in the states. It was a marvelous place to embrace nature.

We flew to India in 1937, and when we returned to England, there was a new King — George the Sixth. He was crowned the same day our son Land was born. Of course, he had the Lindbergh dimple. *(Pause.)* You know, a year later, we met the King and Queen at a ball.

(Curtsies. To Queen.) Yes, Your Majesty, I did have a baby on Coronation Day. Afterward, I woke up and could hear

people still cheering in the streets for you. *(Pause.)* His name is Land. Thank you. When he gets older, I'll tell him you asked about him. *(Pause.)* Yes, Your Majesty, we like it here very much. *(Curtsies. To audience.)* The Queen even asked Charles to dance, but he had never danced in his life, so he declined. *(Happy.)* I danced until I was giddy; Charles had never seen me so happy. *(Pause.)* Things had turned around and the dance of life was very satisfying.

(Goes to bench, stage right.)

We made a trip to the States in November that year. *(To Charles.)* Oh Charles, I'm glad we celebrated Christmas with the children before we left, but maybe we were gone a bit too long this time. Listen to Jon — he talks with an English accent! And Land is just a baby; we've been gone half of his life. If we hadn't had our portraits done in New York, we could have been home weeks ago. *(Pause.)*

Soon after that, we moved to Illiec, a remote island off the coast of France. We had an old stone house with no heat, no electricity and no plumbing. But it was a compelling setting. We were surrounded by water, so we had to come and go with the tide. We lived with all the phases of the moon — and felt its constant pull and control of our lives. *(Pause.)*

It was during this time that Charles became more and more interested in the struggles between European nations. Because of his aviation expertise, ambassadors and air attaches asked for his technical assessment of air power. For Britain, he assessed Russian aviation. For America and France, he assessed German aviation. He believed Germany was stronger than England and France combined.

War was the hottest topic at so many of the social functions we attended, and the discussions often got quite heated. Charles agreed with many people that peace through negotiation was the best solution. He became more and more engaged in politics, and because he still had a hero's status, we began to easily move in and out of diplomatic social circles.

(Goes to stage center.)

You might have heard about the medal Charles received from the German government. Yes, the Service Cross of the German Eagle. He came back that night and handed it to me. *(To Charles.)* The Albatross. *(Pause.)* Oh Charles, this will haunt you forever. Yes, I know the new Ambassador used you as bait to get the Germans to our embassy for dinner. And I understand he wanted to improve relations with Germany. But he should have warned you about this medal. *(Back to audience.)* He could be so stubborn. For years, friends urged Charles to return it, but he refused. Said he didn't return any of his other medals. *(Pause.)*

(SIIL goes to chair at center stage.)

By the time we returned to the States in 1939, Charles was

──────────────── *Shells* ────────────────

quite excited about his new mission. General Hap Arnold asked him to help assess and develop the country's aviation program. And I supported him, not only in what he did, but in what he believed. I thought that was my duty as his wife. But it took him from home for extended periods — and it caused me great personal pain to take on his beliefs.

Charles agreed with more than eighty percent of the American people that we shouldn't go to war. He thought that war takes away the best young men a country has. Which is true, of course. *(Pause.)* His real fear, though, was that the Soviet Union and communism would take over Europe, and he feared the Soviets more than he feared the Germans. So he began to denounce intervention, even though ultimately it was a hopeless cause.

The Roosevelt Administration didn't want him to speak out. They even offered to form a special cabinet position for him — Secretary of Air — if he didn't. Well, Charles flatly refused that offer. That's when his personal war with President Roosevelt began.

Charles spoke to the public through radio talks and speeches for nearly two years, eventually working with America First. *(Stands. Amused.)* One day we learned the FBI had tapped our phones. So Charles instructed everyone at America First to *(Speaks clearly.)* speak very clearly so they could be well understood. He was a real draw for the rallies. Some people even talked about him running for president of the United States. But Charles

─────────── *Shells* ───────────

wasn't a politician. He was a crusader, so he kept giving speeches all over the country — and was too stubborn to ever change what he wanted to say.

(Comes downstage.)

Even before his famous speech in Des Moines, people began questioning his allegiances and labeling him as anti-Semitic. But after that speech. . . . Oh, my. I'll never forget it. September 11, 1941.

(To Charles.) Charles, I know you want to talk about who you think is pulling the U.S. into the war. And certainly the Roosevelt administration is headed that way. And the British want help. *(Agitated.)* But to say the Jews are pulling the country into the war — why, it would be anti-Semitic. And to rouse anti-Semitism is much worse than war. Oh, Charles! This will be the albatross of speeches! This whole situation is profoundly distressing to me.

(To audience.) He just didn't see it. A very stubborn Swede, he was. The response from that speech was immediate and harsh. He was no longer the great American hero. *(Pause.)*

But he didn't care about public opinion. He only listened to himself. Such stubbornness! Blindness, really. He was blind to whatever he didn't want to see. And I took on his beliefs, so I was just as unseeing. *(Pause.)* I didn't love him any less for all of that, but I pitied him. I *pitied* him. *(Pause.)* It was painful for me to have people see something in him that I didn't. And it didn't all compute for me. I know he made those statements, but I didn't think he was anti-Semitic because I knew him. And I thought I knew what he really believed.

(Goes over to bench, stage right.)

I've thought a lot about all of this over the years. It was terribly stupid. Of course the larger mistake was to get involved in politics at all. We were so naïve. *(Pause.)*

After Pearl Harbor, Charles immediately supported the country's war efforts. He wanted to contribute in the best way he knew how — through aviation. But the Roosevelt administration was still angry with him for all those speeches, so kept him from being hired by a number of companies. *(Pause.)* Henry Ford wouldn't let anyone tell *him* who to hire. So, Charles went to work on producing the B-24 — and we moved to Detroit. *(Amused.)* You can imagine the day President Roosevelt visited the Ford plant — Charles made himself rather scarce.

Things changed, and after a couple of years, Charles was allowed to do what he loved. Fly. He flew fifty combat missions in the South Pacific. Not officially, of course. Officially, he was an observer. His real contribution was teaching the P-38 pilots better fuel consumption, which greatly improved their operations. Charles loved the action — and the men he worked with. *(Pause.)*

The war and the many years of events leading up to it had

Shells

a profound effect on me. I was in my next twenty-year stage. I had more children, published more books, and stayed at Next Day Hill between at least a dozen moves. If all that doesn't introduce you to Real Life, I don't know what does. *(Pause.)* I traveled extensively with Charles. For every trip I took with him, he took three or four more. I wanted to support my husband. I thought that's what a wife should do, and after all, my life evolved around him. *(Pause.)* But my marriage stretched me and changed me so it was not possible to change back.

(Goes to center stage. Pause.)

They say that when two people fall in love and get married, they become as one. The problem is: which one do they become? *(Long pause.)*

I'm afraid I took on Charles' thoughts and ideas without fully understanding my own. It separated and alienated me from so many people I cared about. While Charles was out giving isolationist speeches, my mother and many of our friends were supporting aid to the allies. And I struggled with my divided loyalties. I now understand that Charles and I were the ones who were isolated. *(Pause.)*

I used my talents to support his causes and beliefs. Oh, I enjoyed writing the books about our survey trips. Unfortunately, I immersed myself in his political world. *(Adamant.)* I never should have written *The Wave of the Future*. It was just a slim little book about the political

Shells

environment — and, goodness knows, I'm not a political person. People misunderstood it, so I wrote an article to explain it, but *(exasperated)* it wasn't clear either. Perhaps I didn't understand *myself* then. The book became a best seller, not because it was loved, but because it was despised. And even though I received many letters of support, looking back, it was a mistake. I had no right to publish that book because I didn't know enough. I was terribly distressed over the whole situation. *(Pause.)*

There were times when I just couldn't reconcile to Charles' philosophy, and I often felt ashamed of some of my arguments. At times, I walked around with this dreaded feeling that I wanted to be forgiven, but I didn't know for what or by whom. Worse yet, I questioned my own ability to communicate. I was afraid I'd never publish another book. *(Pause.)*

While Charles was in the Pacific, I was alone to manage my life and my family for the first time. I began to flower and grow. I established life-long friendships with all kinds of artists. *(Excited.)* I took sculpting classes at the Cranbrook Art School. A creative activity is a wonderful way to lose yourself in something . . . to look at things differently. . . and help you find your own identity. I went for walks in the woods. I came out of my shell and learned what I could do alone. I wrote *The Steep Ascent* and sent it to the publisher — against Charles' best judgment. It's a long essay describing a woman's *spiritual* flight. It was another bestseller. *(Pause.)*

─────────── *Shells* ───────────

Charles always said he wanted me to be more independent, more confident. *(Stands up straighter.)* Well, he came home to a different woman. The irony is — he didn't *really* want me to be more independent. *(Pause.)*

The war was finally over, and I entered the next 20-year phase of my life. Active middle age. *(Laughs.)* And was it ever. We moved to Connecticut, and, finally, finally, we bought a home of our own. I'd been married seventeen years, and at long last I had a place I loved and could call my own. Oh, it was a grand place. It's just across the way from here. Unfortunately, once we were settled, Charles took flight. *(Pause.)*

(Goes to chair, center stage. Pours tea.)

He was gone constantly. We didn't know where he went or when he'd return. We only knew he would be gone a few weeks. Between the Air Force and Pan Am, he circled the globe many times each year. Somewhere along the way, I realized that for years I tried to keep up with his pace, but I just couldn't anymore, so I gave up. Oh, Charles, where are you! *(Pause.)*

(Gets indignant.) I was angry and insulted he wasn't there to help me with the children. *(Chuckles.)* I was also relieved when he wasn't there to constantly monitor and scold all of us. *(Pause.)*

My writing is enormously important to me, and so are my children. Many people believe I had only one child

Shells

and wrote only one book. But I gave birth to six children and thirteen books. *(Amused.)* I'm not sure which was more painful. *(Pause.)*

Back in those days, women spent more time in the hospital or in bed after childbirth. My average stay was well over two weeks. Much wasn't known or done about postpartum depression then — that despair and distress familiar to so many women. It's such a contradiction: great depression — just after giving life. *(Pause.)*

Oh, I remember that first time I gave life. *(Chuckles.)* I was afraid the baby would look like my side of the family — with dark hair and a nose all over its face. But then I saw little Charles, with that little dimple in his chin! He was definitely a Lindbergh. *(Pause.)* I had five more children. That's a lot of postpartum! *(Pause.)*

(Goes to stage left.)

Charles called our family a nonbenevolent dictatorship. There's a lot of truth in that. He bullied us all to tears. And even when he wasn't home, the children felt his oppressive presence — and were apprehensive about his return.

When he did return, he sat each child down and went over their individual list. Oh, those lists! He carried them in his briefcase so he could work on them when he traveled. *(Sternly.)* There were rules to be observed, chores to do, and policies to be followed. Unfortunately, their meetings

Shells

often included one of his morality lectures on responsibility or providence or the demise of civilization. *(Smiles.)* The children lived somewhere between juvenile hall and a lecture hall. But he did care about them. *(Pause.)*

(To Charles.) Oh, Charles, I know you care about the children, but couldn't you just allow them a comic book or two? And we're the only house in the neighborhood that doesn't have candy around. Yes, I do think they all enjoyed the slumber party to watch the stars. Yes, they always enjoy our water fights at the dinner table. But Charles, do you have to pour the entire pitcher over someone to begin it? And why do you put a stop to it just when everyone's beginning to really enjoy themselves? Well, I'm not sure they appreciate the flying lessons. That's your candy — not theirs. *(Pause.)*

Charles wasn't sentimental. We didn't celebrate Father's Day or Mother's Day. Although when he was gone on Mother's Day *(Smiling),* the children celebrated it for me. He missed a graduation, a wedding, and a couple of Christmases. When I had knee surgery and really needed him, he was nowhere to be found. *(Looks up, hands out.)* "Where are you, Charles. I *need* you." *(Pause.)*

(Goes to center stage.)

Unfortunately, during this time I often suffered greatly from depression, and not just postpartum. It's a terrible disease, really. You feel anxious. Hopeless. The lack of concentration is terrible for a writer. So often, I felt like a

Shells

failure. Or worthless. It drains your energy and crushes your soul. I've experienced depression many times in my life, and worked my way through and out of it in different ways. Early on, of course, I wrote. That's how I got through the kidnapping. *(Pause.)*

In the fifties, I went to my brother's doctor. Charles was glad Dwight was finally getting good care for his mental illness, but he was furious with me for going to the same doctor for my depression. It was such a relief for me to talk to someone who would simply listen — that I just cried for nearly two years. I felt so separated from life, real or otherwise. I toggled back and forth from May Day — the celebration of spring I enjoy so much — to mayday — the pilot's signal of distress. *(Pause.)* I was angry with myself for putting up with Charles' intolerable behavior. I can only imagine what impact all this had on the children, then and later in their lives. *(Pause.)* We all make choices in life, don't we? *(Pause.)*

Charles and I didn't have a normal social life. You know, dinner with friends, neighborhood parties, that sort of thing. But I've developed wonderful friends over the years. We have shared experiences — and I can count on them. Dr. Dana Atchley has been a trusted friend ever since he helped me through a miscarriage and a gallbladder operation in 1946. He connected with me as no one had before. He understood me in ways that Charles couldn't even begin to imagine — even something as simple and wonderful as daily communication. For years we exchanged little notes — and had friendly visits. Dana

Shells

didn't try to tell me what to do — or what to think. He was a gentle soul.

In the mid-fifties, our friendship grew into a full-grown love affair. It still amazes me how easily I fell into it. It seemed so — natural. We shared long walks, the theater, dry martinis, and for a couple of years, a charming little apartment in New York City. I'm not proud of it, but it gave me daily companionship and affection. My goodness, there's nothing like a romantic interest to pull you out of the depths of depression! *(Amused.)* Actually, I think it works quite well.

I finally called off the affair part of our relationship. Dana protested passionately, of course, but I just couldn't deal with the guilt and lies. And then I felt guilty for leaving *him*. *(Looks over to photos.)* I carry his image in my heart. I grew from that experience. I realized I couldn't find my identity from a love affair, nor could I find it in my marriage. I had to find it myself. *(Pause.)*

My experiences in those years taught me what I could do alone. And it turns out, it was quite a lot! I had always adapted to Charles' life, doing what he expected, going where he wanted. I needed to find my essential self — the person I was before marriage and children, and the person I would be when they left me. And it was so natural that I found it through writing.

(Goes to desk, stage left.)

Shells

In the fifties, Charles and I both experienced writing success. He had his book . . . and I had mine. During the war, he began writing his second book about his flight to Paris. It was published in 1953 — *The Spirit of St. Louis*. He even dedicated it to me: *(Dramatically.)* "To A.M.L., who will never realize how much of this book she has written." *(To Charles.)* Yes, Charles, I do know how much of that book was mine. I helped make it so successful — because I made it better. Remember? I spent countless hours editing the book and provided the poetry of those Pulitzer prize-winning pages. Of course I'm happy for you. *(Sits. To audience.)*

I was also jealous. An interesting emotion for the devoted wife, don't you think? I've always thought that Charles learned a lot about writing from me. After all, that was *my* world, and *I* took *him* on that flight.

The book made Charles happy, and for a while he possessed a generosity of spirit I seldom saw. So the Christmas of 1953 was truly one of our happiest. I recorded it in my diary: *(Picks up book. Robust.)* "Boom days are here again. The Great Man — The Great Epic — The Great Author. I am living in the aura of 1929 again. *(Pause. Pensively.)* Only . . . I am different…." *(Pause. Stands.)*

When I first met Charles, I thought of myself as his page, a willing attendant to his needs. I thought I could play the role of page until I grew up. Well, I did grow up. It happened over a number of years, of course, starting with my time alone during the war. I struggled to find myself, my

———————————— *Shells* ————————————

world. *(Smiles.)* Well, I finally did find my voice. And it wasn't the voice of a radio operator — or a page. *(Pause.)*

It was *my* voice, and it was strong — with my thoughts, my ideas. It was my struggle with Real Life that led me to write *Gift from the Sea*. Perhaps you've read it? *(Smiles.)* Oh, yes, thank you. Well, I was fragmented by all those family responsibilities, surrounded by small children and trying to work out my own problems. So instead of using my craft to talk about flying or politics, I used it to share my thoughts and experiences with others who were also trying to make sense of their lives.

The book grew out of my trips to a place called Captiva. I believe everyone *must* take time for themselves. So for years, I've gone there for a few weeks to shed that winter chill in the warm Florida sun. Now there are some gratifying walks. And I love the simplicity of that little seashell of a house. Sometimes I have a friend with me. I love it when my sister Constance comes to visit.

(To Constance.) Oh Con, remember that marvelous week we had together one winter? We fixed seafood and salads. You found all those perfect moon shells. We walked under the stars and went back and sipped sherry. One night we talked almost all night. Another, we hardly said a word. It was the perfect dance. *(To audience.)* Aren't we lucky to have wonderful people around us to share life's constant stream of love? *(Pause. To center stage.)*

I'm still astonished, and naturally gratified, by how

―――――――――――――― *Shells* ――――――――――――――

my book touched so many people over so many years. People searching for their own identity, trying to work out their own problems. There was such a great response to the book because there were a lot of frustrated women. *(Laughs.)* I guess there still are. Some things never change. *(Pause.)*

The book was an immediate success, and has been ever since. Unfortunately, Charles was out of town extensively that year, so he didn't have to live with *my* success. He supported my writing, he just didn't always support me. Where were you, Charles! *(Pause.)* So, I finally had my book too. I find it amusing that it's now listed under religion in bookstores. Religion. I'm the one who feeds the birds for my daily prayers. *(Laughing.)* But my Presbyterian mother would be proud.

(Goes to bench, stage right. Picks up photo with Thor.)

You know, there's one family member I always remember with great love and affection. After the kidnapping, Charles wanted protection for the family, so we got Thor. Here he is, a beautiful German Shepard. Thor went with us wherever we lived — New Jersey, Long Island, Detroit — he even went to England and France. *(Laughs.)* He probably didn't really appreciate the Queen Mary.

Thor was considered *my* dog, but Charles trained him. He taught him to open and close doors, to take me by the wrist to the kitchen, or to take messages between Charles and me. Oh, lots of tricks. And *(whispers)*, he taught Thor

─────────────── *Shells* ───────────────

to do all of those things from the command of a whisper. *(Back to normal voice. Amused.)* Charles thought he could train the children the same way.

(With affection.) Thor was a loyal and faithful friend, providing protection and companionship for all of his days. *(Pause. Puts photo down.)* If only some people could be more like our animal friends. *(Pause.)*

Thor is buried in the woods near our house in Detroit. Charles dug the grave before Thor died because he was leaving town and we knew the end was near. He died that same day. *(Pause.)*

(Goes to stage center.)

In Hawaii it's considered bad luck to have your grave dug before you die. But in 1974 — after more than a year of fighting cancer — that's exactly what Charles did. Even in death he was in control. He directed everything, including the flight from New York to Hawaii. We weren't sure he would live through that flight, but he was willing to risk it. If you think about it, it would have been a fine death for Charles — to die in the air.

(To Charles.) Oh Charles, I'm so glad we made it to Hawaii. I know you love it here. It's gratifying to have our three sons with us. Yes, they're working through all those specifications on your lists, even the most difficult ones. Yes, everything. The coffin. The grave. The headstone. The service. Charles, why did you tell Land to not let me

Shells

spend a lot of time defending you? I don't understand. *(To audience.)* Charles was buried within hours of his death — and before the press got wind of it. He had finally outwitted the stalkers. *(Pause.)* A part of me died that day.

(Pause. Lights down. Spotlight on Anne.) "And life is eternal, and love is immortal, and death is only a horizon, and a horizon is nothing save the limit of our sight…." *(Pause. Lights return.)*

(Walks to stage right.)

Even on his deathbed, Charles was awfully disagreeable, displaying that anger that was so familiar to us. For years, I was often the target of it. During the kidnapping trial, he said I neglected my work of writing. He didn't speak to me for months when I started seeing a psychiatrist. He scolded me for writing letters to friends. He dismissed me when I thought I had the chicken pox. Turned out I did. *(Smiles.)* He believed me when he caught them. *(Pause.)*

(To Charles.) Oh Charles! After just these few years, I still feel married to you. I feel our marriage goes on, even after death. I'm always aware of how you would approach things or see things. Even now.

(To audience.) Charles loved our house in Hawaii because it was so secluded. We named it Argonauta — the unusual and delicate shell the mother and young ones live in for a while — and then abandon to start other lives.

———————— *Shells* ————————

(Goes to chair, center stage.)

I much prefer my little shell of a house in Switzerland. I call it Planorbe — the French word for that wonderful, small Moon Shell. It's the one that reminds me of the necessity for solitude. I still spend time there every year. In fact, I'm leaving next Tuesday for a few weeks at Planorbe. It's a wonderful place to think — and to write. I need to think about this next twenty-year phase of my life — the abandoned shell.

(Goes to windows, closes curtains.) Oh, excuse me, I must draw the drapes. I don't want anyone watching. *(Returns to center stage.)*

Switzerland is a wonderful place for walks, or just gazing at the broad valleys and steep mountains. You can hear the church bells — and cowbells — in the distance. *(In background: Bach's Orchestral Suite No. 3, Air.)* And the clear, night sky gives you a marvelous look at the moon, the stars and the constellations. I can still pick out the familiar patterns, especially the Navigator's Circle. *(Looks up, points around.)* Capella, Castor, Pollux, Procyon, Sirius. . . . Oh, it's grand.

I spend a lot of time out on my balcony gazing at the stars. It's where I feel closest to Charles now, connected really, so it's where I communicate with him — without words, but with great emotion. Just as sure as the stars blaze clearly in the night sky, I believe those who have passed on, blaze within us. *(Pause.)*

Shells

Well, I must go pack. *(Goes to desk, picks up paper.)* I have my list here somewhere. Ah, here. Yes, I've enjoyed our visit too — sharing our lives. Yes, I do think we have a lot in common. Perhaps I'll see you when I return? I hope so. *(Pause.)* Good night now.

(Music comes up. She picks up tea service, exits. Lights down.)

End of Act One

Act Two

SCENE I: *The stage is the same. It's September 1980.*

(Music begins. Beethoven's 9th Symphony, second movement, first 90 seconds. Lights come up. Anne enters, stage left, puts tea tray on table, center stage, and puts shawl on chair.)

ANNE. How nice to see you again. It's that time of day, so I've made us some tea. There's such a chill in the air. Oh, I do love the fall. One can take such gratifying walks. *(She sits. Pours tea.)*

I've been going for a lot of walks recently. It's so good for the soul — to be with nature. It's always nice to get back here to my little place at Scott's Cove. Every day, I watch the pull of the moon take the tide out and bring it back in. The forces of nature renew my spirit and remind me that the cycle of life continues — no matter what happens to us. *(Pause.)* I'm very fortunate because I've had so many places in my life where I've been able to enjoy a wonderful relationship with nature.

―――――――――――― *Shells* ――――――――――――

Yes, I've just returned from Switzerland. Now there are some gratifying walks. My little house on the side of a mountain has marvelous panoramic views of the valley, and at night, there's an endless sea of stars. It offers a wonderful perspective for one's life.

I love the simplicity of that house — and the solitude it offers. Planorbe — my own little moon shell. There are fewer distractions there, so it's a good place to think about one's life. And of course I think about Charles. It's a wonderful opportunity, in a way, when a man dies. You can see all the different periods of his life. It offers a different perspective. On this trip, I thought a lot about Charles — and our life together. *(Pause.)*

I've also been listening to a lot of music lately. Oh, music can soothe the soul, don't you think? It's a touchstone, really, and can restore so much in you. I can be in a crowded concert hall and still feel a solitary communion with the music. It's the only thing that makes me stop fearing death and age.

I remember when we returned from Europe, Charles went out and bought a Victrola and surprised me with a record of one of my favorites — Beethoven's Ninth. And Bach, oh Bach puts me in a state of grace — that inner spiritual harmony. Music gives me that inner place where all losses are restored and sorrows end, where the things I believe in are still true. *(Pause.)*

(Goes to center stage. Paces.)

Shells

I don't know if I should tell you this, but I have to talk with someone. Shortly after I arrived at Planorbe, I was looking for a particular book. I looked everywhere. It's a small place; not really large enough to store a lot of unwanted items. Charles hated the accumulated possessions of life. I ended up downstairs in a guest bedroom, where I seldom go. Well, I looked on the bookshelf, the dresser, the nightstand. Then I went to the large closet. Way in the back among the extra linens, I found the book. Right next to Charles' old, large briefcase. This was very unusual because Charles always had everything in its place. *(Pause.)*

A briefcase to Charles was so much more than a briefcase. It was a suitcase, an office, a library, a drug store. He never wanted to check a bag when he traveled, so he packed his briefcase instead. Sometimes he would meticulously weigh all the items so it wouldn't go over twenty pounds. He took two of everything in clothing, and he had these inflatable hangers to do laundry.

For good measure, he would carry his disguise — a beret and eyeglasses. *(Amused.)* You never know when you might run into a reporter. And, of course, he had all of those lists buried in there. It was quintessential Charles: practical and efficient. But it was unlike him to leave it in that closet, so I was startled to find it. I took it upstairs to look inside, rather excited, thinking I would feel some unexpected and welcome connection to him. After all, he's been gone six years. And, he's never ceased to surprise me. *(Pause.)* Even now. *(Pause.)*

———————— *Shells* ————————

Well, I found some clothing, stationery, a few maps, a tin of shoe polish. *(Begins to look puzzled.)* And then . . . I saw a large envelope, so I opened it. At first, I couldn't tell what all that was. Some letters postmarked Munich, a few photos. They didn't register with anything familiar to me. *(Confused.)* I just couldn't understand what I was looking at. It was all so . . . unfocused.

(As though looking at photos in hands.) The photos didn't make any sense. There was Charles in that silly beret. But who were those small children around him. He was in some of the photos, so it did register that he must have known the children. Somehow. Where was he? What, what was I seeing? So, I started to read one of the letters. *(As though has letters in hands.)* And, well, it didn't make any sense either. *(Pause.)*

(Slowly.) And then . . . and then it came to me. It was like a small airplane going into a stall — then turning into an out-of-control, spiraling nose-dive right into the earth. More terrifying than any flight I'd ever experienced. Oh Charles! I think I'm going to die. I looked at the photos again — at those small children. And there it was, looking back at me. *(As though holding photos up. Pause.)* That unmistakable — *unmistakable* — Lindbergh dimple in the chin. *(Pause.)*

I sat down in total disbelief. I was dazed and nauseated — as though someone had punched me in the stomach. I couldn't breathe. I was turned inside out and upside down. That distress call over and over in my head —

──────────── *Shells* ────────────

mayday, mayday, mayday. The airplane was breaking up and all I could think was, "Oh Charles! Oh, Charles! How could you!" *(Pause.)* As I started to pull out of the dive, clarity began to circle my mind and — life came back into focus. So many things became clear. In that moment, I realized I'd been flying blind for years. *(Pause. Takes deep breath.)* Then I fixed myself a very dry martini — and sat down. For a long time. *(Goes to bench at stage right and sits. Pause.)*

When I felt grounded enough, I read the letters. How could I not? *(Picks up, reads letter.)* Dear C: You hadn't been gone one day when the children began asking when you'd return. . . . We can't wait until your next visit. *(Looks up.)* This was a whole different life for Charles. Another *life*. Another *family*. Nothing practical or efficient about that! At first I was in total disbelief. Then, as if lightning hit that airplane, I understood so much more about Charles.

Indescribable anger consumed me — as I had never experienced before. I was outraged. I felt humiliated. And foolish. *(Pause. Looks at letters.)* Let's see. We're so glad to be in our new house. . . . I'm thankful the children will be going to good schools now. As I've said so many times, I'm eternally grateful to you for providing us with so much. . . . We all miss you and send our love. Brigitte. *(Pause.)*

The photos show three children — two boys and a girl. The names and dates were on the back. I can only guess they were born from the late fifties into the sixties. *(Pause.)*

Shells

I do remember in the early sixties that Charles took on additional responsibilities in Europe with Pan Am. When his uncle needed nursing care, Charles put him in a home in Switzerland. And he *volunteered* to join the board of the World Wildlife Fund, headquartered in Switzerland. *(Indignant.)* Wildlife, indeed! *(Pause.)*

After I refreshed my martini, a flood of questions rushed over me. Of course, I wondered how and why all this came about. And I wondered what kind of relationship he had with Brigitte. But who was I to point a finger? Did Charles know about Dana Atchley? He certainly didn't say anything. Was it in retribution? That wouldn't be like Charles. But then, right now, I couldn't say for sure what he was like. Here I always thought he was true north, like the star. And I find out he was headed south. And, as with a child, once you find out he's been telling lies, you question everything else he's said or done.

I suspected other women over the years. I even found some letters once, a photo another time. But nothing like *this*. This isn't just another woman, this is another family. Another life. And, those children were born well beyond my own childbearing years. *(Indignant.)* Oh, Charles, how many lives and families did you have! How could you!

(Pause. Stands.)

It set me to thinking. Can I justify my own affair more because it was just that? Or was my relationship with

Shells

Dana the same as Charles' affair? Clearly it lasted as long, perhaps longer. I'll need a lot of walks and music to think this through.

(Speaking to Charles' photo.) Oh, Charles. It appears we each went our own ways about the same time. If you had found out about Dana, would you have been disappointed? Or relieved? If you did know about him, then certainly you knew I called it off. But you didn't. We both insulted each other, took away each other's dignity. But the one thing we always had for each other — respect — what happened to that? Did we look the other way? *(Pause.)*

And did you leave the envelope on purpose for me to find? You were always so meticulous. They say there are no mistakes in life. I wondered about that myself when I lost my wedding ring sometime in the fifties. Is *your* lost briefcase *my* lost wedding ring? And you had the audacity to publish a book with the title *Autobiography of Values*. Oh, Charles! *(Pause.)* What was your personal truth? I spent my whole life trying to define who I am and be true to that. Oh, I made plenty of mistakes along the way, but I always came back to my personal truths. And you were at the heart of all of that. And now my heart feels such pain I can hardly stand it. *(Pause. Back to audience.)*

(Paces back and forth.) I don't know what I would have done had I found this out before Charles died. I'm faced with this truth only now, so that's all I have to deal with. Of course, I wish I had never found out, but denial is impossible now, as much as I'd like to cling to it, especially since

Shells

I've obviously been so good at it. But if I had to find out, I'm glad it was after he was gone.

Charles only listened to himself, and he believed he was never wrong. He never gave back the Albatross. And, he didn't think it was wrong to practically abandon his family for so many years. *(Agonizing.)* So if I had found out about another family in another country, I just may not have liked his response. I know I've carried the burden of guilt about my affair; I'm not sure Charles did the same. And how on earth do you re-establish that trust? *(Pause.)*

It's certainly ironic. It was Charles who told me never to put anything in writing I wouldn't want seen on the front page of a newspaper. And here were love letters. Letters of love. To *my* husband. *(Adamant.)* My hero. *(Pause.)* Well, I burned all the letters and photos in the wood above. But are there more? I could only destroy what I had. Of course, now I'll quietly go through everything, hoping the children never find out. *(Pause.)*

(To Charles.) Oh Charles! What about those children in the photo? Do they know who their father is? After all, you were once the most photographed man in the world. Surely they've seen photos of you somewhere. What will they think? More importantly to me, what would *our* children think if they knew they had these siblings? What if they find out?! Oh, Charles! And what about our children as your living witnesses — offering perspective about your life? Providing a shining example of living life with integrity and honor. How does that work now? *(Pause.)*

―――――――――――― *Shells* ――――――――――――

We were always worried about everyone else trying to tell The Charles Lindbergh Story. We hated to hear that another biography was being written. It was one thing when people got the facts wrong, but it was entirely something else when they questioned your *integrity*. *(Adamant.)* I never wanted your integrity to be in doubt. And now the worst has happened. *I* question your integrity.

(Pause. Goes to center stage.)

I remember after my first baby was kidnapped, I was distraught. But I worked very hard to resist hatred. I've always felt that, with a tragedy, a part of you dies. And, surely another part of me has died. But a good thing about life is that, if you're strong, you can be born many times. That's what happened nearly fifty years ago, and I hope that's what will happen now. *(Pause.)*

Marriage is about sacrifice. I remember writing very early on that it wasn't about happiness. How prophetic I was. Charles expected me to follow him and I did. Around the country and around the world. I thought it was my duty as a wife to go with him and support him in every way. I wanted us to share the same life — the same dreams. Looking back, I probably wouldn't have traveled as much. Not left my babies as much. But I submerged my own feelings to be with him.

(Pause. To Charles.) Charles, what were you looking for with another family? What were you getting from them that you weren't getting from us? Another best friend?

Shells

Did you want to be the hero all over again? To another woman, other children? Or — were they the perfect family for you? No expectations. No commitments. No questions. I wonder what you really thought about my book *Dearly Beloved*. (*Pause.*)

(*To audience.*) The book is about love and relationships and was published during the same time Charles was having this other family. The setting is a wedding ceremony. The parents of the bride suffered through many problems over the years, but they stayed together. People wondered why.

Early on in life, I thought losing a child was amputation. Later, I thought divorce was amputation. A part of you is taken away — never to be reconnected. Divorce disconnects so many things: communication with a shared life and its memories — and the basis for security within a family. I believe that love is a continuous stream in life — and the flow shouldn't be obstructed or cut off. (*Trails off.*) And, I guess I've always liked being a Lindbergh. (*Pause.*)

(*Goes to bench, stage right. Music fades in. Bach's Concerto in D minor for oboe, strings and basso continuo, Adagio.*)

Charles used to tell our children that my silence could be devastating. Could it ever! He *knew* when I was angry by my silence. It was a way of putting up with his mood swings, verbal assaults, and rantings against the children and me. (*Amused.*) With lots of practice, I became quite

Shells

good at it. But I'm not sure I could be silent enough with this. In Switzerland, I couldn't bring myself to communicate with him from the balcony. It was painful to even look at the stars. And the moon I always loved so much. Is it just a cold rock?

(Puts photo of Charles face down on table. Goes to window, closes curtains.)

Well, here it is — Real Life. How much more real can it get? And just when it slams right into me, it all seems so *unreal*. Even surreal. Fortunately, I have my home here to provide a safe place and allow me to reflect on my life now. The perfect shell of protection to guard against the outside, and perhaps even the realities of life.

(She sits in chair, center stage. Lights down.)

Shells

SCENE II: *Same setting. November 1980.*

(*Music continues. Lights up. ANNE is at window, looking through binoculars, searching.*)

ANNE. I thought I spotted that red squirrel. Yes. There. There it is, just under the copper beech tree. Oh, it's delightful.

(*Puts down binoculars, comes forward to center stage.*)

(*Smiles.*) I've often thought how convenient it would be if you could find your true center just by looking through binoculars for the inner self. I spent a lot of time over the years, looking inward for myself and my world. It's hard work to become a whole person, to develop and understand your own heart, your mind and your true spirit. Especially since it's a continuous process as life changes. While I spent a good amount of time in Charles' world of action, I think I found my own place in the world. Oh, it included Charles and the children, but it also included my world of books and poetry and art. And I found many wonderful friends in those worlds.

Now I'm looking ahead to the next phase, the next twenty years of my life. It's totally different now. For one thing, it's difficult being alone. I've always said that the cure for loneliness is solitude. (*Smiles.*) Well, I have as much as I want or need these days. I ought to be permanently cured.

Shells

(Pause. Goes to writing desk, stage left. Picks up tablet.)

I'm planning a trip to Florida and was just working on my packing list. I've been going there now for nearly 50 years. I love those luxurious walks on the beach. They'll help me think about my future writing projects.

For so many of us, writing every day sharpens our powers of observation and expression. It helps us breathe. It's part of our bliss. *(Pause.)* Writing allows me to see things more clearly — to find a more authentic place within myself. It's not easy to give yourself the gift of time for your own inward journey.

When I was young, I wrote because I was shy and couldn't talk in front of people. I admired Virginia Woolf, and I agreed with her that you must have a room of your own as well as money. She thought they give you power — to think for yourself, and about your life and the world. Of course, I had my own money. And, wherever I was, I arranged for that room of my own.

(Sits in chair at desk.)

I created many special places to write. After the kidnapping, I had to get away from the intensity of my mother's house, so I rented an apartment in New York City. Just for writing. And, oh, I needed to write — to find my way out of grief. That's when I wrote *North to the Orient* — shortly before we moved to Europe.

─────────── *Shells* ───────────

That very first room made me realize it was my protective cover, my writing shell. Like the refuge of the cockpit. My room was my place where my time and thoughts were my own. I was protected from the outside world — the children needing me, Charles admonishing me for something. In the process of writing, when you experience that moment of insight, you must attend to it. All my special rooms allowed me to do just that. *(Pause.)*

In England, I had a room set aside in the large house at Long Barn. It overlooked the beautiful gardens and fields. That's where I wrote *Listen! the Wind*. I had a similar room in our home in France, but it overlooked the rocks and the ocean.

When we moved to Long Island, I wrote in a part of the garage that had a wonderful expansive view of the sound. *(Laughing.)* With the help of two maids, a nurse and a cook, I was able to go to my special room and really focus on my writing.

You see, it's not just taking the time to sit and write. You have to cut out the rest of your world and concentrate on your work. And, that's not easy. At another home, I used a charming little playhouse on top of a hill. On Martha's Vineyard, I had a large tent. I even put up curtains. Sometimes Charles and I slept in that tent.

(Goes to center stage.)

In Detroit, Henry Ford gave us a small trailer from the

--- *Shells* ---

Edison Museum, and we put it in the back yard. Although I had written most of *The Steep Ascent* prior to the war, I pulled it all together in that little trailer.

After the war, I took it with me to Connecticut. I went to Europe for two months to talk to the people and write about their spiritual renewal. Well, in that little trailer I wrote a number of magazine articles.

Then we moved to Darien and I had my own writing room upstairs. Later, I had a tool shed we put behind the house. When we moved into this smaller place, I had the whole house, so I didn't need a trailer or a garage or a tent or a tool shed. *(Points to desk upstage.)* I enjoyed using my father's desk — there.

At our home in Switzerland, *(Looks up.)* I have a little mini-chalet further up the hill. The view is so expansive that even your thoughts can take flight.

(Goes back to writing desk, sits.)

In all of my special rooms, I surrounded myself with meaningful items: prints of paintings, pictures of angels, feathers, driftwood — and always shells. *(Picks up shells. Light over shoulder up. Motions to light coming over left shoulder)* And, I had to have that clear light coming over my left shoulder. My sharp pencils curled the blue paper as I wrote. Charles and the children knew the rules. There were to be no interruptions. But occasionally one of the children needed something. *(Smiling.)* I think they

Shells

showed great courage when they came and knocked on that door. Charles had his own way of getting my attention. He would stand around the corner and whistle — and I would always go to him. *(Pause.)*

I became another person when I wrote. I forgot my children, I forgot my husband — it's a terrible conflict, really. I was constantly choosing between those that I loved and that which I loved to do. My own room helped me keep the focus I needed to separate myself from the activity around me, and concentrate on the words in front of me. To find clarity. *(Pause.)*

(Stands.) One of my favorite writers is the German poet Rilke. He understood the need for solitude — and the ultimate aloneness of man. And, he knew we should not be presumptuous about each others' lives. *(As Rilke.)* "Do not believe that he who seeks to comfort you lives untroubled among the simple and quiet words that sometimes do you good…. Were it otherwise, he would never have been able to find those words." *(Pause.)* Indeed. *(Pause.)*

(Goes to center stage.)

I've just completed my thirteenth book, the fifth book of letters and diaries. They convey the story of my personal journey. *(Smiles.)* Of course, some of my very early writings are quite naïve — writings of an inexperienced and innocent young woman. But, taken together, I think the books tell the story of that young woman coming out from the protective shell of home and parents. I believe

―――――――――― *Shells* ――――――――――

I was very open and honest about some of the most difficult times in my life: my successes and failures — the heights of my happiness and depths of my depressions. And, I think the books convey my continuous quest to find Real Life. *(Smiles. Pause.)*

I've had wonderful support for my writing over the years. From family and friends, from my publishers. Even my writing teacher from Smith always encouraged me. Charles was always supportive. But he never understood my difficulty in constantly changing back and forth from my outer world to my inner thoughts. He thought it was easy — like flipping a switch.

We oftentimes helped each other in our work. Just days before his death, Charles gave the draft of his *Autobiography of Values* to his publisher, Bill Jovanovich. So I helped him with it. *(Rather amused. To Bill.)* Bill, I didn't realize that Charles neglected to talk about his children — in his autobiography! Oh, yes, he mentioned a couple of the boys, but barely. It seems to me that a book of values should surely include one's children. Here. *(Shows photos.)* I've brought you photos of our six children, all identified; you must include them. They were lovely children. *(Pause.)*

(Goes to bench at stage left. Sits.)

Someone else contributed greatly to my writing. The French aviator Antoine de Saint-Exupery. Also known as St. Ex. Now *there* was communion — a true spiritual fellowship. He was a pilot and a writer. But not just a man

Shells

of words. He was a man of *emotions*. He understood the inner life — the spiritual journey.

We even shared Rilke as a favorite poet. St. Ex. wrote *Wind, Sand and Stars*, and said everything I would ever have wanted to say about flying and time and human relationships. Yes, that's right. He did write *The Little Prince*. Oh, he understood relationships. I've always agreed with his thought that love does not consist in gazing at each other... but in looking outward together in the same direction. St. Ex. thought that above all else, one should consciously affirm life. *(Enthusiastically.)* Embrace life! *(Pause. Stands.)*

I met him once. Only once. But our connection was like summer lightning — and made an indelible impression on my life. He wrote the introduction to the French version of my book, *Listen! the Wind*. It showed such insight and sensitivity to me and my writing — naturally I wanted to meet him.

He came to visit one August evening before the war. He didn't speak English, but he spoke my language better than anyone I've ever met. *(Smiling.)* And, thank goodness I spoke French. We had the same thoughts, the same love of poetry. We talked all evening — with great intensity and understanding. Finishing each other's sentences. In French! And he had this wonderful sense of humor. It was so exciting! *(Pause.)*

The most important thing about that evening was that he

———————— *Shells* ————————

talked to me about my craft — our craft — of writing. He respected my work, and me as a writer, and he wanted to fence with my *mind* — steel on steel. Well, I was smitten!

You see, I've spent a great deal of my life as the sideshow. *(Very animated puts hand out as if to shake, while looking over shoulder as if looking at Charles.)* So often, someone would meet me and while shaking hands with me, look over their shoulder at Charles. "Hello, how do you do?" I was dismissed outright. But St. Ex. was interested in *my* thoughts and *my* writing — not an image of someone . . . or someone's wife. *(Pause.)*

When I published *The Steep Ascent*, I thought of it as a letter to him. He was the *one* person who would truly understand that spiritual journey. But I don't even know if he read it. Sometimes I felt I was writing just for him, because he would have recognized the soul of the writing — and the writer.

But he was fighting in the war, and certainly did not agree with the position Charles and I had taken. At first, I was excited when I wrote *The Wave of the Future* because I was sure he would understand. But very few people understood that book. I didn't feel I could even contact him again. I watched carefully for any news about him when he returned to France to serve his country.

When he was reported missing, I was hit with that familiar sharp pain of the realization of death. Every day — over and over. Just as with the baby and Elisabeth. To think of living in a world without his humanity and compassion was almost unbearable. *(Pause.)*

I bristle when people liken Charles' work in *The Spirit of St. Louis* to the works of St. Exupery. They're not the same. Charles' book is worthy, but it lacks the love and compassion of the books of St. Ex. He was a star who illuminated our earth, and his death was a great loss to the light of the world. St. Ex. has been part of my inner journey all these years. Surely an intellectual affair. And I think he lived the true definition of a hero. *(Pause.)*

(Goes to center stage.)

I've thought a lot about the notion of a hero — and being a hero. F. Scott Fitzgerald said, "Show me a hero and I'll write you a tragedy." *(Pause.)*

I've heard that word practically my whole life. After all, I was a hero worshiper. Remember? I wanted to marry a hero. But over the years, I've thought about heroes, and what a hero is — or should be. *(Pause.)*

I did marry a hero. Charles' flight to Paris catapulted him right into hero status. It certainly was a risky adventure way beyond the ordinary for 1927. And, he was a hero for aviation at a time when it needed a champion, someone to promote the virtues of flight we take for granted today. But over the years, I think we all made too much of Charles as a hero. *(Pause.)*

------------------ *Shells* ------------------

St. Ex. was a different kind of hero. He made the ultimate sacrifice for his country, but he was also a hero for his spiritual journey. A journey that took him to a place within himself. And, oh, he wrote about it like an angel. It's the journey we are all on, to find our inner self. And no matter how much the outer world changes over the years, our inward life and our quest to find out who we are remains the same. St. Ex. understood this. *(Pause.)*

Does one become a hero because of one event — or a lifetime? I believe it can be either. I also believe a person can lose that hero status — like a fallen angel. *(Amused.)* Hmmm. A fallen hero. Some people are heroes just by the way they live their daily lives. Caring for the people around them, people who bear witness for those daily unheroic actions. We all know heroes — perhaps we don't always recognize them, and they seldom recognize themselves. Like that red squirrel. *(Pause.)*

(Goes to chair, center stage. Sits.)

There were many times in my life when I took an experience and rededicated myself to the life I knew and had nourished — my husband, my family, and my craft of writing. Meeting St. Ex. on that August night was one of those experiences. *(Pause)*

Throughout my life, I struggled to meet the expectations of others. Now, with my husband gone and my children scattered, I understand I should dedicate myself — *to*

Shells

myself. To re-find my center of gravity. And at seventy-four years old, I have no time to waste. *(Pause.)*

Widowhood is another stage of life — the last of those twenty-year cycles, and very different from the previous ones. No one needs me. Not really. That's why I call it the abandoned shell: the Argonauta. Everything I've done up to this point makes it easier to deal with this new stage, but it's still very difficult. It requires a reorientation to once again find the center of gravity of one's life. This final lesson of learning to be independent is the hardest one of all. *(Pause. Stands.)*

But there are compensations. I feel closer to people and more compassionate. Maybe I just realize that you and I are so much alike. We have similar experiences, just different stories. Possessions are no longer as important and become some of life's baggage that can be shed — like taking excess weight out of Tingmissartoq to cross the Atlantic.

I spend a lot of time in this stage thinking about life in my other stages. I think about my relationships with family and friends. Relationships are everything, and they can be so complex and difficult. We demand too much from them. It's not easy to balance the dance of a relationship — sometimes a waltz, sometimes a tango. Intermittency plays a big part. We don't love someone in the same way all the time. Every season, every year. And we dare not grasp someone too tight. The music might stop.

Shells

And so I've wondered if I was too devoted to Charles. A young naïve woman, abandoning my children and taking on my husband's beliefs. Was I too much of a protective shell for my own family? Oh, we Lindberghs are good at protecting each other. But where do you draw the line? We all have our own truths in life, and now I'll have to live with the new truths of mine.

I've had a few months to think about the greater truths of Charles — and my life with him. You can never regret the past or call it a waste. And while time gives us the opportunity to think about people and relationships, I think we should also think about the constants in life — like the moon that pulls on us or the stars that guide us. For nearly fifty years, Charles was the most constant element in my life. We shared families, children, writing and flying. *(Smiles.)* Remember, I had the sky!

I still have a lot of long walks to take, a lot of music to experience, and a lot of birds to feed to be in that harmonious state of grace again, but I know one thing. While the relationship changed over the years, the powerful personal connection we had was inexplicable — and it still is. And that remains one of my constant — and comforting — truths.

I also now understand why Charles told one of our sons to not let me spend much time defending him. And, indeed, I don't feel like defending him as much as I have. I felt the same way when I gave up on trying to keep up with his schedule. I do think he would be devastated by my

———————— *Shells* ————————

silence this time. And I don't know how long this silence will last — or if I'll ever be able to go out on that balcony and share the stars with him again. *(Pause.)*

I've also had some time to think more about my lengthy relationship with Dana. Oh, the affair lasted only a couple of years, but we maintained a caring relationship well before and after the affair years. I'm grateful he has always been there for me emotionally — with a call, a visit or a note. Sometimes women's true needs are so simple, don't you think? *(Pause. Goes to center stage.)*

(Cheerful.) Of all my relationships, some of the ones I treasure the most now are with my grandchildren. Oh, what a joy. Grandchildren are more seductive than anything else in life. Mine call me Grannymouse. Grannymouse. Isn't that charming?

So Grannymouse now lives a simple life here at Tellina, my house named after the Double Sunrise shell. It's a shell for old age. It offers shelter and protection — and shields me from the outside world. I can manage my own life in as much solitude as I want, or can stand.

Here I experience the comforting cycle of nature — death and rebirth. Yes, I've experienced many re-births — perhaps more than I'd like. But tragedies can make you stronger. *(Pause.)* Did you know that if a starfish loses an arm, a new one will grow in its place? Or if it's cut in half, each half can become a new starfish? So if half of you is taken away, you can still grow and mature. Imagine —

Shells

actually become stronger from amputation. We can learn so much from nature.

(Goes to bench at stage right. Sits.)

In the world I was desperately trying to find, I was on a constant search for Real Life — a life without all those protective shells. Especially the one of privilege. Over the years, there were many things I thought were Real Life. Charles brought me Real Life, a life of action. *(Amused.)* Certainly children come with a large dose of reality. *(Pause.)* But I didn't need to go looking for Real Life — it found me. Death is real. And despair. Surely disappointment. But fortunately, so are babies and books and birds. And music. Oh, so many joys of life. Sometimes Real Life is just being alone with one's thoughts. *(Pause.)*

It was the journey that brought Real Life experiences in and out of my life, the same way the moon takes the tide in and out every day. It's the journey that matters. For me, it's both an inward and outward journey. And my soul is where they meet.

Part of the journey is letting go. To a great extent, you have to let go of your loved ones when they die. Not that you'll forget them, you just have to accept that change in your life. I've lost so many people who were close: my parents, my sister, my first son, my husband. I remember when we lived on that rugged island off the coast of Brittany. The roar of the sea and howling of the wind made me restless at first. The longer I was there, the more I began to feel

Shells

it was very much like life, that in order to find complete peace, you had to let go in it. Like giving in to the bank of an airplane and just enjoying it. As St. Ex would say, "Choose life!" *(Pause.)*

(Walks to center stage.) I'm so looking forward to my trip to Florida. I can't wait to take that first walk on the beach and enjoy the solitude — and perhaps find a few shells. Have you ever noticed how only the nicest, most perfect shells are picked up? How *do* we survive that turbulent trip to the beach?

My walks are usually alone. After all, ultimately we are all alone. But we always carry inside ourselves those who have gone before us. I agree with Rilke that some of the best things in life are invisible — like love, friendship, memories, or a bird's song.

(Remembers. Goes to chair, picks up shawl, goes to desk, picks up basket.)

Oh my goodness, the birds. It's time for me to go to church and pray. To offer up my cracked corn and breadcrumbs. I think about a lot of things on my walks. I've been wondering what a *Gift from the Sea* for old age would be like. If you look back on your whole life and what it means, do you become more open, more honest? Do you give in to your truths more? And can you easily share that with others? As though you're just sharing tea and cookies? Surely a lot to think about. *(Goes to center stage.) (Pause.)*

I'm grateful for my life and all the friends I've made along the way. I still think communication is one of the most exciting things in life, especially with good friends. *(Pause.)*

Years ago when I first traveled with Charles and was just about the most shy person in the world, I discovered I truly enjoyed going around the country with him and meeting all kinds of people and sharing experiences — learning about the journeys of others. I've never been comfortable talking about myself. Still, I very much enjoyed our time together. Thank you for the connection and communication.

As you know, in my family an experience was not finished until it was written down or shared in some way. It's the experience of being alive. I'm very happy to have shared this experience with you. *(Smiles.)* And, I'll enjoy it again as I write about it in my diary. Good-bye for now.

(Music comes up. Bach, Brandenburg Concerto No. 3. Exits, stage left.)

The End

About the Author

Virnell Bruce spent 36 years in the aerospace industry before she decided to fulfill her dream of writing a one-woman play on Anne Morrow Lindbergh. This was something she wanted to do ever since 1985 — when she read *Bring Me A Unicorn* about the same time she saw *Lillian*, a one-woman play by William Luce on Lillian Hellman.

Virnell gives presentations on Mrs. Lindbergh as well teaches a class through the Christopher Wren Association in Williamsburg, which is the education program for people over 55 years old sponsored by the College of William and Mary.

She has a Master's Degree in Journalism from the University of Southern California and also holds a Bachelor's degree in English. She lives in Williamsburg, Virginia, with her cat Annie.

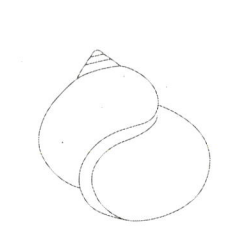